Madge & Tim
& the children

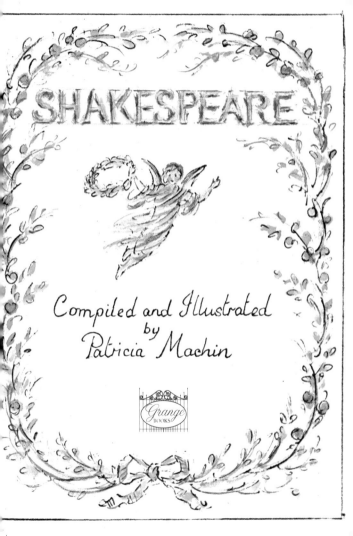

SHAKESPEARE

Compiled and Illustrated
by
Patricia Machin

Grange
BOOKS

Published by Grange Books
An Imprint of Books and Toys Limited
The Grange
Grange Yard
London SE1 3AG

ISBN 1 85627 265 6

This edition reprinted in 1993

First published in Great Britain
1985 by Webb & Bower (Publishers) Limited
9 Colleton Crescent, Exeter, Devon EX2 4BY
Copyright © 1985 Webb & Bower (Publishers) Limited

Typeset in Great Britain by P&M Typesetting Limited,
Exeter, Devon.

Printed in Spain by
Graficas Reunidas

Contents

Introduction

William Shakespeare, the eldest son of John and
Mary, daughter of Robert Arden, a farmer from an
old county family, was born at Stratford-on-Avon in
1564. Occupations such as butchery and wool dealing
are attributed to his father who held various
municipal offices and owned property, but by the
time William was thirteen he had lost his wealth and
also that of his wife.

It is significant that Shakespeare was born into an
age of momentous achievement. The unparalleled
discoveries concerning the universe, the exploration
of new lands, the rediscovery of the great classical
period forgotten during the Middle Ages, and the
increase of printing created the right environment for
the full development of a great talent. It is not
surprising, therefore, that this Elizabethen age was to
be known as the English Renaissance.

Little is known of Shakespeare's childhood. His
marriage to Anne Hathaway is recorded in 1583, also
the birth of a daughter and then a twin son and
daughter, and it is possible that at this time he was a
schoolmaster. In 1587 no fewer than five companies
of players visited Stratford and this may have proved
irresistible to Shakespeare for he left his family and

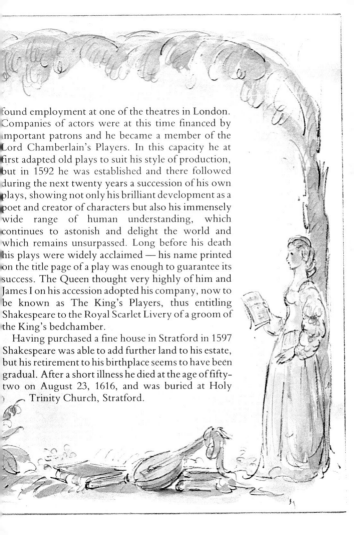

found employment at one of the theatres in London. Companies of actors were at this time financed by important patrons and he became a member of the Lord Chamberlain's Players. In this capacity he at first adapted old plays to suit his style of production, but in 1592 he was established and there followed during the next twenty years a succession of his own plays, showing not only his brilliant development as a poet and creator of characters but also his immensely wide range of human understanding, which continues to astonish and delight the world and which remains unsurpassed. Long before his death his plays were widely acclaimed — his name printed on the title page of a play was enough to guarantee its success. The Queen thought very highly of him and James I on his accession adopted his company, now to be known as The King's Players, thus entitling Shakespeare to the Royal Scarlet Livery of a groom of the King's bedchamber.

Having purchased a fine house in Stratford in 1597 Shakespeare was able to add further land to his estate, but his retirement to his birthplace seems to have been gradual. After a short illness he died at the age of fifty-two on August 23, 1616, and was buried at Holy Trinity Church, Stratford.

This poem was written as a song for the play *Two Gentlemen of Verona*; it was the first of many exquisite songs Shakespeare wrote for his plays. The play was probably written in 1594-5 and the plot is said to have been based on the popular pastoral romance *Diana Enamorada* by the Portugese poet Jorge de Montemayer (1521-61). This work was extremely popular and was translated into English, German and French.

Silvia

WHO is Silvia? What is she?
    That all our swains commend her?
Holy, fair, and wise is she;
    The heaven such grace did lend her,
That she might admirèd be.

Is she kind as she is fair?
    For beauty lives with kindness:
Love doth to her eyes repair,
    To help him of his blindness;
And, being help'd, inhabits there.

Then to Silvia let us sing,
    That Silvia is excelling;
She excels each mortal thing
    Upon the dull earth dwelling:
To her let us garlands bring.

These lines, known as 'The Cuckoo Song', precede the poem 'Winter' at the end of the comedy *Love's Labour Lost,* an early play probably first produced in 1595.

The accounts for the Master of the Revels for the Christmas season 1604-5 are preserved and show that at least seven (including *Love's Labour Lost*) of the eleven plays presented at King James I's court were by Shakespeare and that they were presented by the King's Men, Shakespeare's own company.

WHEN daisies pied and violets blue,
   And lady-smocks all silver-white,
And cuckoo-buds of yellow hue
   Do paint the meadows with delight,
The cuckoo then, on every tree,
Mocks married men; for thus sings he,
         Cuckoo!
Cuckoo, cuckoo! – O word of fear,
Unpleasing to a married ear!

When shepherds pipe on oaten straws,
   And merry larks are ploughmen's clocks,
When turtles tread, and rooks, and daws,
   And maidens bleach their summer smocks
The cuckoo then, on every tree,
Mocks married men; for thus sings he,
         Cuckoo!
Cuckoo, cuckoo! – O word of fear,
Unpleasing to a married ear!

This poem represents the closing verses of *Love's Labour Lost*, one of a set of plays that show Shakespeare in his youth, light-hearted and exuberant and yet technically the complete master, changing frequently from rhyme to prose and then to blank verse. The poem's wonderful pictorial power has produced a perfect miniature of England in winter at that time.

WHEN icicles hang by the wall,
   And Dick the shepherd blows his nail,
And Tom bears logs into the hall,
   And milk comes frozen home in pail,
When blood is nipp'd and ways be foul,
Then nightly sings the staring owl,
                  To-whot!
To-who!–a merry note,
While greasy Joan doth keel the pot.

When all aloud the wind doth blow,
   And coughing drowns the parson's saw,
And birds sit brooding in the snow,
   And Marian's nose looks red and raw,
When roasted crabs hiss in the bowl,
Then nightly sings the staring owl,
                  To-whit!
To-who!–a merry note,
While greasy Joan doth keel the pot.

'Come Away Death' is considered one of Shakespeare's most beautiful songs. It is sung by the clown in *Twelfth Night* a comedy in which the humour is provided by the minor characters, Sir Toby Belch, Sir Andrew Aguecheek and the pompous Malvolio. It was presented to the Queen in the Great Hall of Whitehall Palace on Twelfth Night, 1601.

Come away, come away, death,
　And in sad cypres let me be laid;
Fly away, fly away, breath;
　I am slain by a fair cruel maid.
My shroud of white, stuck all with yew,
　　O prepare it!
My part of death, no one so true
　　Did share it.

Not a flower, not a flower sweet,
　On my black coffin let there be strown;
Not a friend, not a friend greet
　My poor corse, where my bones shall be
　　　　　thrown:
A thousand thousand sighs to save,
　　Lay me, O, where
Sad true lover never find my grave
　　To weep there!

Sonnets

Much has been written about Shakespeare's sonnets with a view to discovering the source of his inspiration. However, as nothing has been proved perhaps it is better to read these exquisite poems (nine of the one hundred and fifty-four are included here) and enjoy their haunting imagery and cadence without troubling ourselves about to whom they were written. Poetry, particularly in sonnet form, was fashionable and very much more highly rated as literature than were plays in Shakespeare's day.

To me, fair friend, you never can be old;
For as you were when first your eye I eyed,
Such seems your beauty still. Three Winters cold
Have from the forests shook three Summers' pride;
Three beauteous Springs to yellow Autumn turn'd
In process of the seasons have I seen,
Three April perfumes in three hot Junes burn'd,
Since first I saw you fresh, which yet are green,
Ah! yet doth beauty, like a dial-hand,
Steal from his figure, and no pace perceived;
So your sweet hue, which methinks still doth stand,
Hath motion, and mine eye may be deceived:
    For fear of which, hear this, thou age unbred:
    Ere you were born was beauty's Summer dead.

WHEN to the Sessions of sweet silent thought
I summon up remembrance of things past,
I sigh the lack of many a thing I sought,
And with old woes new wail my dear time's waste:
Then can I drown an eye, unused to flow,
For precious friends hid in death's dateless night,
And weep afresh love's long-since-cancell'd woe,
And moan th' expense of many a vanish'd sight:
Then can I grieve at grievances foregone,
And heavily from woe to woe tell o'er
The sad account of fore-bemoanèd moan,
Which I new pay as if not paid before.
   But if the while I think on thee, dear friend,
   All losses are restored and sorrows end.

THAT time of year though may'st in me
                    behold
When yellow leaves, or none, or few, do hang
Upon those boughs which shake against the cold—
Bare ruin'd choirs where late the sweet birds sang.
In me thou see'st the twilight of such day
As after Sunset fadeth in the West,
Which by and by black night doth take away,
Death's second self, that seals up all in rest.
In me thou see'st the glowing of such fire
That on the ashes of his youth doth lie,
As the death-bed whereon it must expire,
Consumed with that which it was nourish'd by.
   This thou perceiv'st, which makes thy love more
                    strong
   To love that well which thou must leave ere long.

O HOW much more doth beauty beauteous seem
By that sweet ornament which truth doth give!
The Rose looks fair, but fairer we it deem
For that sweet odour which doth in it live.
The Canker-blooms have full as deep a dye
As the perfumèd tincture of the Roses,
Hang on such thorns, and play as wantonly
When summer's breath their maskèd buds discloses:
But—for their virtue only is their show—
They live unwoo'd and unrespected fade,
Die to themselves. Sweet Roses do not so;
Of their sweet deaths are sweetest odours made.
    And so of you, beauteous and lovely youth,
    When that shall vade, my verse distils your truth.

BEING your slave, what should I do but tend
Upon the hours and times of your desire?
I have no precious time at all to spend,
Nor services to do, till you require.
Nor dare I chide the world–without–end hour
Whilst I, my sovereign, watch the clock for you,
Nor think the bitterness of absence sour
When you have bid your servant once adieu;
Nor dare I question with my jealous thought
Where you may be, or your affairs suppose,
But, like a sad slave, stay and think of nought
Save, where you are how happy you make those!
   So true a fool is love, that in your Will,
   Though you do any thing, he thinks no ill.

How like a Winter hath my absence been
From thee, the pleasure of the fleeting year!
What freezings have I felt, what dark days seen,
What old December's bareness everywhere!
And yet this time removed was summer's time;
The teeming Autumn, big with rich increase,
Bearing the wanton burden of the prime
Like widow'd wombs after their Lord's decease:
Yet this abundant issue seem'd to me
But hope of orphans and unfather'd fruit;
For Summer and his pleasures wait on thee,
And, thou away, the very birds are mute:
   Or if they sing, 'tis with so dull a cheer
    That leaves look pale, dreading the Winter's near.

FROM you have I been absent in the spring,
When proud-pied April, dress'd in all his trim,
Hath put a spirit of youth in everything,
That heavy Saturn laugh'd and leap'd with him.
Yet nor the lays of birds, nor the sweet smell
Of different flowers in odour and in hue,
Could make me any summer's story tell,
Or from their proud lap pluck them where they grew;
Nor did I wonder at the Lily's white,
Nor praise the deep vermilion in the Rose;
They were but sweet, but figures of delight,
Drawn after you, you pattern of all those.
   Yet seem'd it Winter still, and, you away,
   As with your shadow I with these did play.

SHALL I compare thee to a Summer's day?
Thou art more lovely and more temperate:
Rough winds do shake the darling buds of May,
And Summer's lease hath all too short a date:
Sometime too hot the eye of heaven shines,
And often is his gold complexion dimm'd;
And every fair from fair sometime declines,
By chance or nature's changing course
                                    untrimm'd:
But thy eternal Summer shall not fade
Nor lose possession of that fair thou owest;
Nor shall Death brag thou wanderest in his
                                    shade,
When in eternal lines to time thou growest:
    So long as men can breathe, or eyes can see,
    So long lives this, and this gives life to thee.

WHEN in the chronicle of wasted time
I see descriptions of the fairest wights,
And beauty making beautiful old rime
In praise of Ladies dead and lovely Knights;
Then, in the blazon of sweet beauty's best,
Of hand, of foot, of lip, of eye, of brow,
I see their antique pen would have exprest
Even such a beauty as you master now.
So all their praises are but prophecies
Of this our time, all you prefiguring;
And for they look'd but with divining eyes,
They had not skill enough your worth to sing:
   For we, which now behold these present
                      days,
    Have eyes to wonder, but lack tongues to
                      praise.

In *Richard II* Shakespeare has portrayed the complex character of a king who was crowned when only a child and all the tragic events of his reign with such power and understanding of his wayward yet endearing personality that it remains one of the most memorable historical plays ever written. The famous soliloquy on patriotism (spoken by John of Gaunt on his death-bed) and two moving speeches by Richard as he faces the horrors of betrayal and deposition are given here.

Methinks I am a prophet new inspir'd,
And thus expiring do foretell of him:
His rash fierce blaze of riot cannot last,
For violent fires soon burn out themselves;
Small showers last long, but sudden storms are
    short;
He tires betimes that spurs too fast betimes;
With eager feeding food doth choke the feeder:
Light vanity, insatiate cormorant,
Consuming means, soon preys upon itself.
This royal throne of kings, this scepter'd isle,
This earth of majesty, this seat of Mars,
This other Eden, demi-paradise,
This fortress built by Nature for herself
Against infection and the hand of war,
This happy breed of men, this little world,
This precious stone set in the silver sea,
Which serves it in the office of a wall,
Or as a moat defensive to a house,
Against the envy of less happier lands,
This blessed plot, this earth, this realm,
    this England.

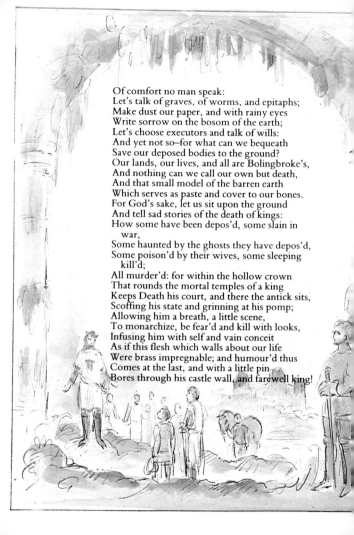

Of comfort no man speak:
Let's talk of graves, of worms, and epitaphs;
Make dust our paper, and with rainy eyes
Write sorrow on the bosom of the earth;
Let's choose executors and talk of wills:
And yet not so–for what can we bequeath
Save our deposed bodies to the ground?
Our lands, our lives, and all are Bolingbroke's,
And nothing can we call our own but death,
And that small model of the barren earth
Which serves as paste and cover to our bones.
For God's sake, let us sit upon the ground
And tell sad stories of the death of kings:
How some have been depos'd, some slain in
        war,
Some haunted by the ghosts they have depos'd,
Some poison'd by their wives, some sleeping
        kill'd;
All murder'd: for within the hollow crown
That rounds the mortal temples of a king
Keeps Death his court, and there the antick sits,
Scoffing his state and grinning at his pomp;
Allowing him a breath, a little scene,
To monarchize, be fear'd and kill with looks,
Infusing him with self and vain conceit
As if this flesh which walls about our life
Were brass impregnable; and humour'd thus
Comes at the last, and with a little pin
Bores through his castle wall, and farewell king!

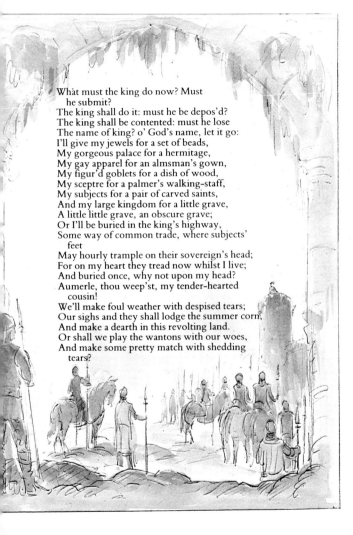

What must the king do now? Must
  he submit?
The king shall do it: must he be depos'd?
The king shall be contented: must he lose
The name of king? o' God's name, let it go:
I'll give my jewels for a set of beads,
My gorgeous palace for a hermitage,
My gay apparel for an almsman's gown,
My figur'd goblets for a dish of wood,
My sceptre for a palmer's walking-staff,
My subjects for a pair of carved saints,
And my large kingdom for a little grave,
A little little grave, an obscure grave;
Or I'll be buried in the king's highway,
Some way of common trade, where subjects'
  feet
May hourly trample on their sovereign's head;
For on my heart they tread now whilst I live;
And buried once, why not upon my head?
Aumerle, thou weep'st, my tender-hearted
  cousin!
We'll make foul weather with despised tears;
Our sighs and they shall lodge the summer corn,
And make a dearth in this revolting land.
Or shall we play the wantons with our woes,
And make some pretty match with shedding
  tears?

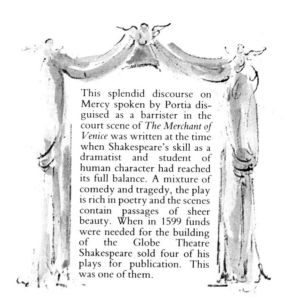

This splendid discourse on Mercy spoken by Portia disguised as a barrister in the court scene of *The Merchant of Venice* was written at the time when Shakespeare's skill as a dramatist and student of human character had reached its full balance. A mixture of comedy and tragedy, the play is rich in poetry and the scenes contain passages of sheer beauty. When in 1599 funds were needed for the building of the Globe Theatre Shakespeare sold four of his plays for publication. This was one of them.

The quality of mercy is not strain'd,
It droppeth as the gentle rain from heaven
Upon the place beneath: it is twice bless'd;
It blesseth him that gives and him that takes:
'Tis mightiest in the mightiest; it becomes
The throned monarch better than his crown;
His sceptre shows the force of temporal power,
The attribute to awe and majesty,
Wherein doth sit the dread and fear of kings;
But mercy is above this sceptred sway,
It is enthroned in the hearts of kings,
It is an attribute to God himself,
And earthly power doth then show likest God's
When mercy seasons justice. Therefore, Jew,
Though justice be thy plea, consider this,
That in the course of justice none of us
Should see salvation: we do pray for mercy,
And that same prayer doth teach us all to render
The deeds of mercy.

These delightful songs are from the comedy *As You Like It*, a play based on Thomas Lodge's romance *Rosalynde*; the music was by Thomas Morley. In 1603, after the death of the Queen, the Jacobean age began inauspiciously with an outbreak of the plague in which 30,000 Londoners died. The theatres were closed and Shakespeare's company went on tour. The Court was at the Earl of Pembroke's home, Wilton House, Salisbury, and there on December 2 Shakespeare and his men gave their first performance before the King. The play was *As you Like it*.

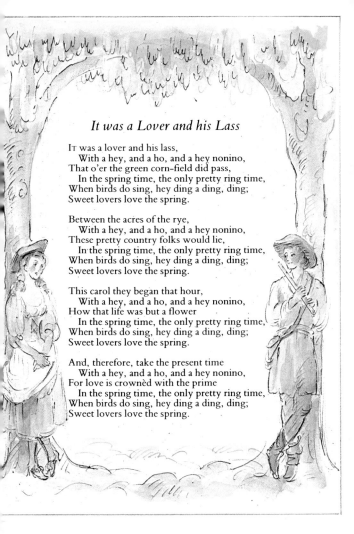

It was a Lover and his Lass

It was a lover and his lass,
  With a hey, and a ho, and a hey nonino,
That o'er the green corn-field did pass,
  In the spring time, the only pretty ring time,
When birds do sing, hey ding a ding, ding;
Sweet lovers love the spring.

Between the acres of the rye,
  With a hey, and a ho, and a hey nonino,
These pretty country folks would lie,
  In the spring time, the only pretty ring time,
When birds do sing, hey ding a ding, ding;
Sweet lovers love the spring.

This carol they began that hour,
  With a hey, and a ho, and a hey nonino,
How that life was but a flower
  In the spring time, the only pretty ring time,
When birds do sing, hey ding a ding, ding;
Sweet lovers love the spring.

And, therefore, take the present time
  With a hey, and a ho, and a hey nonino,
For love is crownèd with the prime
  In the spring time, the only pretty ring time,
When birds do sing, hey ding a ding, ding;
Sweet lovers love the spring.

Under the Greenwood Tree

Amiens sings:
UNDER the greenwood tree,
  Who loves to lie with me,
And turn his merry note
Unto the sweet bird's throat,
Come hither, come hither, come hither:
    Here shall he see
    No enemy
But winter and rough weather.

Who doth ambition shun,
And loves to live i' the sun,
Seeking the food he eats,
And pleased with what he gets,
Come hither, come hither, come hither:
    Here shall he see
    No enemy
But winter and rough weather.

Jaques replies:
  If it do come to pass
  That any man turn ass,
  Leaving his wealth and ease
  A stubborn will to please,
Ducdamè, ducdamè, ducdamè:
    Here shall he see
    Gross fools as he
An if he will come to me.

Blow, blow, thou Winter Wind

BLOW, blow, thou winter wind,
   Thou art not so unkind
    As man's ingratitude;
Thy tooth is not so keen,
Bacause thou art not seen,
    Although thy breath be rude.
Heigh ho! sing, heigh ho! unto the green holly:
Most friendship is feigning, most loving mere folly:
    Then heigh ho, the holly!
    This life is most jolly.

Freeze, freeze, thou bitter sky,
   That dost not bite so nigh
    As benefits forgot:
Though thou the waters warp,
Thy sting is not so sharp
    As friend remember'd not.
Heigh ho! sing, heigh ho! unto the green holly:
Most friendship is feigning, most loving mere folly:
    Then heigh ho, the holly!
    This life is most jolly.

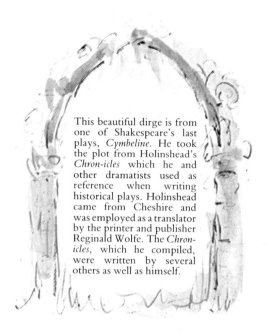

This beautiful dirge is from one of Shakespeare's last plays, *Cymbeline*. He took the plot from Holinshead's *Chron-icles* which he and other dramatists used as reference when writing historical plays. Holinshead came from Cheshire and was employed as a translator by the printer and publisher Reginald Wolfe. The *Chron-icles*, which he compiled, were written by several others as well as himself.

Fidele

FEAR no more the heat o' the sun,
  Nor the furious winter's rages;
Thou thy worldly task hast done,
  Home art gone, and ta'en thy wages:
Golden lads and girls all must,
As chimney-sweepers, come to dust.

Fear no more the frown o' the great,
  Thou art past the tyrant's stroke;
Care no more to clothe and eat;
  To thee the reed is as the oak:
The sceptre, learning, physic, must
All follow this, and come to dust.

Fear no more the lightning-flash,
  Nor the all-dreaded thunder-stone;
Fear not slander, censure rash;
  Thou hast finish'd joy and moan:
All lovers young, all lovers must
Consign to thee, and come to dust.

No exorciser harm thee!
Nor no witchcraft charm thee!
Ghost unlaid forbear thee!
Nothing ill come near thee!
Quiet consummation have;
And renownèd be thy grave!

When Shakespeare was at the
height of his powers he applied
himself to the writing of
tragedies; they were written
between 1600 and 1608 and, to
the enrichment of English speech,
Hamlet has been more quoted
than any other play. The famous
reflective speech by Hamlet
himself, the Queen's vivid and
poetic description of Ophelia's
death and the timeless wisdom
imparted by the aged Polonius to
his son in memorable verse are
the three excerpts illustrated here.

Yet here, Laertes! aboard, aboard, for
  shame!
The wind sits in the shoulder of your sail,
And you are stay'd for. There, my blessing with
  thee!
And these few precepts in thy memory
Look thou character. Give thy thoughts no
  tongue,
Nor any unproportion'd thought his act.
Be thou familiar, but by no means vulgar;
The friends thou hast, and their adoption tried,
Grapple them to thy soul with hoops of steel;
But do not dull thy palm with entertainment
Of each new-hatch'd, unfledg'd comrade. Be-
  ware
Of entrance to a quarrel, but, being in,
Bear't that th' opposed may beware of thee.
Give every man thine ear, but few thy voice;
Take each man's censure, but reserve thy judg-
  ment.
Costly thy habit as thy purse can buy,
But not express'd in fancy; rich, not gaudy;
For the apparel oft proclaims the man,
And they in France of the best rank and station
Are most select and generous, chief in that.
Neither a borrower, nor a lender be;
For loan oft loses both itself and friend,
And borrowing dulls the edge of husbandry.
This above all: to thine own self be true,
And it must follow, as the night the day,
Thou canst not then be false to any man.
Farewell; my blessing season this in thee!

To be, or not to be: that is the question:
Whether 'tis nobler in the mind to suffer
The slings and arrows of outrageous fortune,
Or to take arms against a sea of troubles,
And by opposing end them? To die: to sleep;
No more; and, by a sleep to say we end
The heart-ache and the thousand natural shocks
That flesh is heir to, 'tis a consummation
Devoutly to be wish'd. To die, to sleep;
To sleep; perchance to dream; ay, there's the rub;
For in that sleep of death what dreams may come
When we have shuffled off this mortal coil,
Must give us pause. There's the respect
That makes calamity of so long life;
For who would bear the whips and scorns of time,
The oppressor's wrong, the proud man's contumely,
The pangs of dispriz'd love, the law's delay,
The insolence of office, and the spurns
That patient merit of the unworthy takes,
When he himself might his quietus make
With a bare bodkin? who would fardels bear,
To grunt and sweat under a weary life,
But that the dread of something after death,
The undiscover'd country from whose bourn
No traveller returns, puzzles the will,
And makes us rather bear those ills we have
Than fly to others that we know not of?

There is a willow grows aslant a brook,
That shows his hoar leaves in the glassy stream;
There with fantastic garlands did she come,
Of crow-flowers, nettles, daisies, and long
    purples,
That liberal shepherds give a grosser name,
But our cold maids do dead men's fingers call
    them:
There, on the pendent boughs her coronet weeds
Clambering to hang, an envious sliver broke,
When down her weedy trophies and herself
Fell in the weeping brook. Her clothes spread
    wide,
And, mermaid-like, awhile they bore her up;
Which time she chanted snatches of old tunes,
As one incapable of her own distress,
Or like a creature native and indu'd
Unto that element; but long it could not be
Till that her garments, heavy with their drink,
Pull'd the poor wretch from her melodious lay
To muddy death.

This lullaby, sung to Titania, queen of the fairies, by her attendants as they guard her while she sleeps is Fairyland itself, recaptured by Shakespeare for all time. When *A Midsummer Night's Dream* was written Fairyland and all its creatures was not dismissed as childish fabrication; spells and bewitchments were reality for the majority of people. This play was performed by the King's Players at the first Christmas revels of James I at Hampton Court in 1603.

You spotted snakes with double tongue,
  Thorny hedgehogs, be not seen;
Newts and blind-worms, do no wrong;
  Come not near our fairy queen.

    Philomel, with melody,
    Sing in our sweet lullaby;
  Lulla, lulla, lullaby; lulla, lulla, lullaby!
      Never harm,
      Nor spell nor charm,
    Come our lovely lady nigh;
    So, good night, with lullaby.

Weaving spiders, come not here;
  Hence, you long-legg'd spinners, hence!
Beetles black, approach not near;
  Worm nor snail, do no offence.

    Philomel, with melody,
    Sing in our sweet lullaby;
  Lulla, lulla, lullaby; lulla, lulla, lullaby!
      Never harm,
      Nor spell nor charm,
    Come our lovely lady nigh;
    So, good night, with lullaby!

This wonderfully descriptive short poem is another from the play *Cymbeline*, written towards the end of Shakespeare's life when he was in semi-retirement. It is sung by Cloten and his musicians in an attempt to entice Imogene (who has secretly married Leonatus) from her room. The historical aspect of the play is freely adapted from Holinshead but the story is of Ginevra from Boccacio's *Decameron*.

Aubade

HARK! hark! the lark at heaven's gate sings,
  And Phœbus 'gins arise,
His steeds to water at those springs
  On chaliced flowers that lies;
And winking Mary-buds begin
  To ope their golden eyes:
With everything that pretty bin,
  My lady sweet, arise!
    Arise, arise!

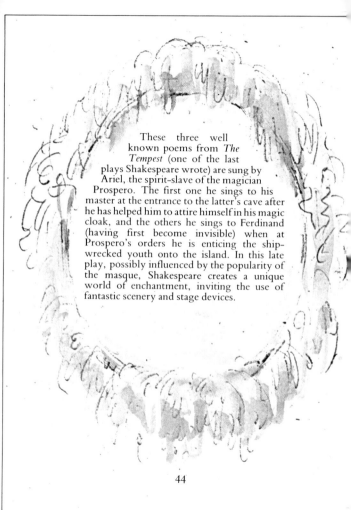

These three well known poems from *The Tempest* (one of the last plays Shakespeare wrote) are sung by Ariel, the spirit-slave of the magician Prospero. The first one he sings to his master at the entrance to the latter's cave after he has helped him to attire himself in his magic cloak, and the others he sings to Ferdinand (having first become invisible) when at Prospero's orders he is enticing the ship-wrecked youth onto the island. In this late play, possibly influenced by the popularity of the masque, Shakespeare creates a unique world of enchantment, inviting the use of fantastic scenery and stage devices.

WHERE the bee sucks, there suck I:
   In a cowslip's bell I lie;
There I couch when owls do cry.
On the bat's back I do fly
After summer merrily:
   Merrily, merrily, shall I live now,
   Under the blossom that hangs
                     on the bough.

Come unto these yellow sands,
    And then take hands:
Court'sied when you have, and kiss'd,–
    The wild waves whist,–
Foot it featly here and there;
And, sweet sprites, the burthen bear.
      Hark, hark!
        Bow, wow,
      The watch-dogs bark:
        Bow, wow.
      Hark, hark! I hear
      The strain of strutting chanticleer
      Cry, Cock-a-diddle-dow!

FULL fathom five thy father lies;
  Of his bones are coral made;
Those are pearls that were his eyes:
  Nothing of him that doth fade,
But doth suffer a sea–change
Into something rich and strange.
Sea–nymphs hourly ring his knell:
                    Ding-dong.
  Hark! now I hear them–
              Ding-dong, bell!